End House

I Talk You Talk Press

Old Secrets – Modern Mysteries Book 2

Copyright © 2018 I Talk You Talk Press

ISBN: 978-4-909733-16-0

www.italkyoutalk.com

info@italkyoutalk.com

All rights reserved. No part of this publication may be resold, reproduced, stored in retrieval system, copied in any form or by any means, electronic, mechanical, photocopying, recording or otherwise transmitted without the prior written permission from the publisher. You must not circulate this publication in any format, online or otherwise.

This is a work of fiction. Names, characters, businesses, organizations, products, places, events and incidents are either the products of the author's imagination or are used in a fictitious manner. We have no affiliation with any existing companies mentioned in this story. Any resemblance to actual persons, living or dead, existing stories or actual events is purely coincidental.

Although the author and publisher have made every effort to ensure that the contents of this book were correct at press time, the author and publisher do not assume and hereby disclaim any liability to any party for any loss, damage, or disruption caused by errors or omissions, whether such errors or omissions result from negligence, accident, or any other cause.

For more information, see the Copyright Notice on our website.

Cover illustration image copyright: © Steve Carter 2013
The photograph of Loch Coultrie is used with the kind permission of Steve Carter (http://www.stevecarter.com).

CONTENTS

End House Character List	1
1. They think I did it!	3
2. A long afternoon	7
3. The strangers in the bar	12
4. Dinner at the pub	15
5. More mystery	19
6. Is anything missing?	23
7. Davie	28
8. The other man	31
9. Alec	36
10. Is anyone there?	40
11. The same man	44
12. James is surprised	47

13. The curse of the Dumbartons	50
14. Walter Ferrington	54
15. End House at night	60
16. I have things to tell you	63
17. Cullen's shame	67
18. Davie's letter	70
19. He didn't do it	73
Thank You	77
About the Author	78

END HOUSE CHARACTER LIST

The Dumbartons

Sarah Dumbarton is a retired school teacher. She lives in an old house near a small fishing village in western Scotland. When she was young, she studied at university in Paris. She fell in love with another student, James Winchester. James disappeared from her life and Sarah returned to Scotland. She married Alec Dumbarton. Forty years later, she met James Winchester again. You can read about their meeting in Italy in book one of the Old Secrets - Modern Mysteries series: *The Blue Lace Curtain*.

Alec Dumbarton worked in a bank. He married Sarah Dundas. He died about fifteen years before the events in this story take place.

Davie Dumbarton is Sarah's brother-in-law. He lives in End House, a very old and mysterious house on the edge of a loch in northwest Scotland.

James Winchester

James is a diplomat. He lives in Rome. He and Sarah fell in love in Paris when they were in their twenties. James had to leave Sarah in Paris because he had a very dangerous job in the British Secret Service. He was delighted to meet Sarah again after so many years. He has come to spend a vacation with her.

The Police

Archie Ross is the top policeman in Scotland. He grew up near the village where Sarah lives. He knows her well. When he was a young man, he and James worked together, so he knows James too.

Peter Duncan is a detective. He lives and works in Oban. He and Sarah played together as children.

Rory McClellan is a junior detective. Peter Duncan is his boss. When he was a child, Sarah was his school teacher.

Other characters

Fiona and Len Muir are friends of Sarah's. They own the pub in the village near Sarah's house.

Walter Ferrington lives near End House. He is very interested in old stories and hidden treasure.

Millie Craig has a bed and breakfast hotel near End House. Her mother and Sarah were best friends. Sarah was Millie's school teacher.

Richard Wilson is an antiques dealer from Glasgow. The police think he might be a criminal, but they have never caught him.

1. THEY THINK I DID IT!

James was singing as he drove his rental car towards Lochgilphead. It was a beautiful day and he felt good. He laughed at himself when he realised he was singing *The First Time Ever I Saw Your Face*. It had been on a cassette tape he bought when he was a student. He had played it over and over again during his last year at university.

On his last night in Paris, he and Sarah had sat on the tiny balcony of his apartment drinking wine and listening to this song. That was more than forty years ago. In all that time he had not seen Sarah until six months ago. They had met again, almost by chance, in Italy. Now Sarah had invited him to stay at her house in Western Scotland for a few days.

He stopped in Lochgilphead and checked his map and instructions; only another 25km. He had emailed Sarah saying he would arrive in time for a late lunch. If he didn't get lost, he would be on time.

---*The house is near the ocean* --- Sarah had written. ---*There are no neighbours. The nearest house is almost a kilometre away. I hope you won't find it too quiet* ---.

He drove on along the coastline. He passed some houses standing alone in windswept gardens. Finally he came to a small village with a shop, a hotel, a church and a few houses. Past the village he started looking for a left hand turn.

---*Turn left by the old fishing boat*--- Sarah's instructions said. ---*Drive about 2km. The house is on the top of the hill. You can't miss it.*---

James saw the house as he drove up the hill. There was a stone wall alongside the road. The house was big, and it was surrounded by a large garden. Then James saw the cars. There were two black vans, two police cars and an ordinary car. They were parked on the side of the road. There were a number of people in the garden.

James was worried. He drove towards the wide gates that led to the house. The gates were shut. James stopped the car. A policeman stepped up to the driver's window.

James lowered the window.

"What has happened?" he asked. "Has there been an accident? Is Sarah OK?"

"You can't stop here, sir," said the policeman. "Please drive on."

"No way!" answered James. "What's wrong?"

"Nothing to do with you, sir," answered the policeman. "Now please, just drive on, or drive back the way you came."

James drove the car to the side of the road. He parked it in front of the police cars. Then he got out of the car and walked back to the policeman.

"I am a guest of the woman who owns this house. I'm going in," he told the policeman.

"No you're not," said the policeman. "Not until my boss says you can. But wait here. He will probably want to talk to you."

The policeman took out his mobile phone and talked quietly to someone. James looked at the garden. There were people in white overalls crawling around on the ground. A woman in overalls was taking photographs. To one side of the house he could see a stretcher. There were other people close to the wall of the house, but there were trees and bushes in the way, so he couldn't see what they were doing.

The policeman stopped talking on his phone and turned to James.

"The boss is busy, but one of the detectives is coming out. Wait here."

"But just tell me what is happening!" James was sure something terrible had happened to Sarah.

A young man in casual clothes came out of the house. He walked up to James.

"I'm Detective Constable Rory McClellan. Could you give me your name please, sir?"

"I'm James Winchester. I'm a friend of Sarah Dumbarton. What has happened?"

The detective didn't answer the question. "And your address?"

James gave the detective the address of his apartment in Rome.

"And I understand that you are a guest in this house," said the detective.

"Well, I will be a guest when you let me go in! I flew from Rome to Glasgow very early this morning. I picked up a rental car at the airport and then drove here."

"So you weren't in Scotland last night?"

"No," answered James.

"Can you prove that?"

James gave the man his boarding pass and the rental car agreement. The detective read the papers carefully.

"So you weren't here yesterday or early this morning?"

"No. Now will you please tell me what has happened?"

"I don't think that's necessary, sir. We have your name and address if we want to talk to you. I suggest you go to Oban, or back to Glasgow, and telephone Mrs Dumbarton. She should be free to talk to you later today."

James was very angry. "Now listen to me!" he shouted.

Just then the front door of the house opened, and Sarah came running out.

"James! James! Thank goodness!"

She ran down the wide path to the gate and opened it. "Come in!"

"Mrs Dumbarton!" shouted the policeman. "You can't invite people in! It's a crime scene."

Sarah ignored him. She turned to the detective.

"Rory McClellan! You can tell your boss that this is still my house and James Winchester is my guest!"

Sarah held James' arm, and walked quickly with him down the path to the front door. The door was open and she took James down a hallway and into a big kitchen.

"Sit down," she said. "I thought you would arrive soon, so I made coffee. I'm not allowed to go anywhere else in the house."

James suddenly felt very tired. He sat down at the kitchen table. Sarah poured coffee and handed him a cup. She sat down opposite him.

"Now, first," said James. "I am delighted to be here, and delighted to see you! But what on earth has been going on?"

Sarah smiled at James. "I'm very pleased you're here. Let me tell you. There was a man's body in my garden this morning. He had been shot."

"Oh, poor Sarah." James reached across the table and took Sarah's hands. "What a terrible shock. Did you find the body?"

"No, No. Jim Rumble. He's a fisherman from down in the village. He came up this morning to bring me some fish. I had ordered it to cook for lunch today. He was walking around the side of the house to the kitchen door, when he saw the body. He came running to the door to tell me. I went out to look. The man had been shot in the back. He was dead. I called the police. They arrived about an hour later. They had to come from Oban. They have been here for hours."

"So you saw the dead man. Did you know him?" asked James.

"He was lying face down, so I couldn't see his face well, but I don't think so," answered Sarah. "He seemed to be about forty years old. He had long black hair, and was wearing jeans, motorbike boots and a leather jacket."

"Which way was the body facing?"

"His head was towards the house. He was just outside the living room windows. Maybe he had been looking in the window. The curtains were open." Sarah shivered and James held her hands more tightly.

"Sarah. Why don't we go out? You can't go anywhere in the house. And it has been a terrible day for you. Why don't we go down to the village? I saw a hotel there. Do they serve lunch?"

Sarah pulled her hands away from James'. She stood up and went to the kitchen window. She stared out at the garden.

"I don't think that's possible. They have been searching the house for guns. You see, the police think I did it!"

2. A LONG AFTERNOON

"Why do they think that you killed the man?" James was angry.

"This is the only house on the hill. If you drive past it, it is another 12km or more until you come to a farm. So they think the man came to see me."

"But why do they think that you killed him?"

"I haven't spoken to Peter Duncan yet. He's the detective in charge. But Rory McClellan, the young detective who talked to you at the gate, thinks I saw the man in the garden and was very frightened. So he thinks I took a gun and went outside and shot him! I have to wait until Peter has time to talk to me. I'm so sorry! This is a terrible start to your holiday!"

"Don't worry about me," said James. "But I am hungry! You said the fisherman brought you some fish. Can we eat lunch?"

Sarah laughed. "Jim Rumble was so frightened, he dropped the fish in the garden! It's been outside in the sun all day. We won't be able to eat it now! How about an omelette?"

"Perfect," answered James.

James watched Sarah as she took eggs, cheese and salad greens from the refrigerator. He looked around the kitchen. It was a nice room. It was very big. The walls were stone and the floor was covered in old tiles. There were glass-fronted cabinets filled with blue and white china. Behind the kitchen bench was a long window. Through the window, he could see a vegetable garden. The table where he was sitting was very big. It looked old too.

"I like this kitchen." he said to Sarah. "You told me this was your mother's family home."

"Yes. She was an only child, like me. She grew up in this house, but she died when I was only two years old. I spent many holidays here with my grandparents. My grandfather was the local doctor. When they died, the house became mine. It was empty for years, but then when Alec died, I came here to live. It's a nice house. I like living here. I hope I will be able to show it all to you soon. There's some white wine in the refrigerator. Would you open it? Even if we can't do anything else, we can enjoy our lunch."

James found wine glasses and a bottle opener. He poured wine for Sarah and himself. Sarah brought the plates to the table. She had made cheese omelettes and a green salad. James was very hungry. He enjoyed his lunch. While they were eating Sarah seemed more relaxed. They didn't talk about the dead man in the garden. They talked about when they had met again in Italy after so many years.

After lunch, Sarah and James washed the dishes and put them away. There was no dishwasher in the old-fashioned kitchen.

James poured some more wine and they sat at the table. Sarah stopped talking. She stared at the table.

"Don't worry," said James. "I am sure everything will be OK."

As he was speaking, the kitchen door opened, and a man about the same age as James and Sarah walked in.

"Sarah. I'm ready to ask you some questions now. Will you come into the living room?" asked the man.

"James, this is Peter Duncan," said Sarah. "He's a senior detective with the police in Oban. He's in charge of this murder investigation."

"Peter, this is my friend James Winchester. I'm sure Rory told you already that he arrived today from Rome. He is here for a holiday."

"Yes, Rory told me," answered the detective. "It seems that you were not here when the man was killed, Mr Winchester. Sarah and I will go into the living room, so I can ask her some questions."

"Sarah will only answer questions if I am there too," said James. "So why don't you sit with us here? You can ask all the questions you want."

"James, it's OK," said Sarah. "Peter grew up in Beautore, the village at the bottom of the hill. When I came here for summer holidays, we played together. I have known him all my life."

"No," said James. "He might be your friend from childhood, but he is still a policeman. I want to be with you."

Sarah sighed. She looked at the detective. "Would that be OK, Peter?"

"It makes no difference to me," he said. "But I have to ask you some personal questions. Maybe you don't want your friend to listen."

"I have nothing to hide," said Sarah. "So sit down here and ask your questions."

James was amazed. He was sure that Sarah had many secrets. He had seen her for only a few days in Italy. Before that, it had been forty years since they had been together. James had many secrets. Maybe he would tell Sarah some of them, sometime. But not yet.

Peter went to the door of the kitchen and shouted for Rory McClellan. The young detective came in and sat down at the table. He had a notebook and an audio recorder

"Can I record this interview?" he asked Sarah.

"Of course," said Sarah.

First, Rory McClellan asked Sarah some questions.

"Your name is?"

"Sarah Maeve Dumbarton."

"And your address?"

"Hill House, Beautore.

"Your age?"

"Sixty-three."

"Are you married?"

"I'm a widow."

"What was your name before you got married?"

"Dundas."

"Occupation?"

"Really Rory! Is this necessary?" Sarah was angry. "I taught you when you were in primary school! Have you forgotten?"

Rory turned the recorder off. "I know Mrs Dumbarton. But I have to ask all the questions. It doesn't matter that I know you, and that my boss knows you. We must have a record."

"OK, Rory, I'm sorry. Turn the recorder on and ask me again."

Rory turned the recorder on.

"Occupation?"

"Retired school teacher."

Then Peter Duncan, the older detective, asked Sarah many questions.

Sarah answered all his questions. But Sarah couldn't tell him anything. She didn't know who the man was. She didn't think she had ever seen him before. She hadn't touched the body. The man had been lying face down, so she hadn't seen his face. She had not heard any noise in the night or early in the morning. She had watched television in the living room until about 10:30pm. Then she had gone to bed. She had listened to music on her iPod until about midnight. She got up at 7:30am. Everything in the house seemed normal until Jim Rumble started banging on the kitchen door and shouting at about 9:00am.

"You are sure you never saw this man before?" asked Peter Duncan.

"Peter, I told you," said Sarah. "I don't think so. But I didn't see much of his face. Do you know who he is?"

"Yes. We found his wallet in his jacket pocket. His name was Richard Wilson. He was thirty-seven. He lived in Glasgow. I've sent that information back to the office. I hope they will be able to tell us more about him soon."

"When did he die?" James asked.

"The doctor thinks he died about midnight. We will know more after the post mortem."

"And he was shot?"

"Yes. Whoever shot him fired from a distance away. We don't know what kind of gun yet, but the doctor is guessing it was a rifle."

"Listen to me," said James. "I know that some of you think that Sarah heard or saw this Richard Wilson. Then she panicked and went and got a gun and shot him. But it doesn't make any sense. If Sarah wanted to shoot him, she would have fired the gun through the window or from the door of the house. If she was so frightened, she would not have gone outside and walked around behind him to shoot him."

"Maybe not," answered Peter Duncan. "But we still have a lot of searching to do. You can't stay here Sarah. I have called Fiona and she's preparing a room for you. He turned and smiled at James. "The pub in the village has a few bedrooms for tourists. I've reserved a room for you as well.

"Now, Sarah. You can't take your car because we have to search it.

But I'm sure this gentleman will drive you down to the pub. I will be there at ten o'clock tomorrow morning to talk to you. Why don't you go and pack a bag and get down to the village."

James looked at his watch. It was five o'clock!

"Come on, Sarah. Pack some things and we'll go."

3. THE STRANGERS IN THE BAR

The pub was in the main street of Beautore. There was a small car park behind it. James parked his rental car and took his suitcase out of the boot. He took Sarah's arm and they walked towards the back door of the pub. The door suddenly opened and a very small woman came running towards them

"Sarah! This is terrible! You poor thing!" She hugged Sarah. "Come in. I've been watching for you ever since Peter called!"

She took Sarah's bag and, still talking, led them into the kitchen. "I couldn't believe it when Jim Rumble came into the bar at lunchtime and told us about the dead man in your garden!

"I'm so pleased you're here! You can tell us everything. And you wouldn't want to stay in your house tonight. Not after there's been a murder!"

They were standing in the kitchen when the woman stopped talking.

"James. This is Fiona Muir. She's Peter Duncan's sister. She and her husband Len own this pub," said Sarah.

A teapot, cups and saucers and a plate of shortbread were laid out on the kitchen table.

"Sit down! Sit down! I'll make the tea," said Fiona.

James and Sarah sat down. Fiona filled the teapot and sat down opposite them.

"Now tell me everything!"

"But Fiona, you probably know more than I do," said Sarah. "I saw the dead man in the garden, but that's all."

"Who was he?"

"I don't know. Peter said his name was Richard Wilson, and that he came from Glasgow."

"What did he look like?"

"He had long black hair. He was wearing a leather jacket."

"Wait a minute," said Fiona. She went out of the kitchen. James and Sarah could hear her shouting, "Len! Len!"

Sarah looked at James and laughed. "You look like you've been hit by a truck!"

"Does she always talk so much?" asked James.

"Oh yes, but don't worry. Fiona is a very nice person. You will get used to her. And she's a very good cook."

After a few minutes, Fiona came back.

"Len says there was a man with long black hair and a leather jacket in the bar last night. He was with another man. The other man was a stranger too."

James was interested. "You should tell the police. Perhaps the other man knows something about the murder."

Fiona sat down and poured the tea. It was very strong. James took a piece of shortbread. It was delicious.

"Yes, I'll tell them. But I can tell you something else. The other man can't have shot him."

"Why not?" asked James.

"Len says the two men had an argument. The man with black hair left the bar. Then the other man drank a lot of whisky. He drank too much. He fell asleep. Len couldn't wake him up. He carried him to the dining room and put him on a bench. He covered him with a blanket. He didn't want him to wake up and go back to the bar. So he locked him in the dining room.

"This morning he was still there. Len gave him a cup of coffee and the man went away. Maybe he knows something, but he can't have been the killer."

James was tired. He had left his apartment in Rome thirteen hours ago. He hadn't changed his clothes, and he needed a shower.

"Fiona," he said. "Do you think I could go to my room? I'd like to have a shower and change my clothes."

"Of course," answered Fiona. "I hope you will be comfortable. We only have five rooms for guests, and we only have one good room. I want Sarah to sleep there. She has had a bad day. I thought you could sleep in one of the other rooms. It's small and old fashioned, but the bed is fine."

"I'm sure it will be fine," said James. Fiona took James upstairs. The room had a low ceiling and a very small window. There was only enough room for a bed and a small table, but it was very clean, and the bed looked comfortable.

"There is a bathroom down the hall," said Fiona. "Sarah's room has its own bathroom, so you will have that bathroom to yourself."

"Thank you. The room looks very nice," said James.

Fiona smiled and went back downstairs.

James opened his suitcase and took out clean clothes. He took the towel from the end of the bed and went to the bathroom. It was old fashioned with the shower over the bath, but the water was hot. James felt much better after his shower. He went back to his bedroom and sat on the bed. He couldn't believe that so many things had happened in such a short time. He was very happy to be in Scotland with Sarah, but he was worried. What had happened? Did the police really believe that Sarah had killed that man?

He heard Fiona's voice. She was showing Sarah her room. Fiona's voice was very loud.

"What a lovely man, Sarah," she was saying. "So handsome. He looks rich too. You should marry him. You've been a widow for too long!"

James listened hard but he couldn't hear what Sarah said.

He heard Fiona's footsteps. She stopped at the door of James' room and knocked.

James got off the bed and opened the door.

"Your meal will be ready in an hour," said Fiona. "Sarah will meet you in the dining room."

James went back to bed and lay down. His eyes closed. He fell asleep.

4. DINNER AT THE PUB

James woke up suddenly. *What time is it? Am I late?* He looked at his watch. He had only slept for forty minutes. He went to the bathroom and washed his face in cold water. He went downstairs. The dining room was between the kitchen and the bar. It was decorated in dark brown. It was dark. There were pictures of mountains and deer on the walls. Sarah was sitting at a small table near the door between the kitchen and the dining room. She had changed her clothes. When James arrived at Hill House she had been wearing jeans and a big pale blue sweater. Now she was wearing black pants with a silk top. The top was patterned in purple and black. She had put on make-up, and was wearing long silver earrings. James walked over to the table. He bent down and kissed her.

"You look beautiful," he said.

"Thank you," Sarah smiled. "This is the first night of your vacation. I thought we should be celebrating."

James sat down. "Is there a menu?" he asked. Sarah laughed. "You have been living in Rome too long. This is a small country pub. Fiona will cook something, and we will eat it. There is no choice."

"What about wine?" James could not imagine eating a meal without drinking wine.

"Don't panic. Fiona has spoken to Len. He will bring something to drink soon."

The door from the bar opened. James got a surprise. Len was a very big man. James thought he must be more than 2m tall. He was also very wide. He was carrying a tray with two wine glasses, two bottles of wine and a bottle opener. He put them down on the table. He turned to Sarah and smiled. Sarah stood up. Len hugged her. Len was so big that Sarah looked like a child. Len patted Sarah on the head and put her back in her chair. Then he started talking. James could not understand him. Len's voice was very soft and he had a strong local accent. James looked at Sarah. It seemed that Sarah could understand. Len stopped talking, patted Sarah on the head again, and went back to the bar.

The door to the kitchen opened.

"I would have cooked something special, but Peter only called in the late afternoon. So I'm giving you the same as I cooked for Len for his dinner. Tomorrow night I'll cook something nicer," said Fiona.

She put two bowls of soup and a plate of bread on the table. "I know it's September, but Len likes soup."

James looked at the bottles of wine. There was a bottle of red wine from Australia and a bottle of white wine from New Zealand.

"Why do they have wine from the South Pacific in Scotland?" James asked Sarah.

"Len knows a lot about wine. He goes to Edinburgh to buy it. He always buys some for me too. The wine will be fine."

James opened the red wine. He poured some for himself and tasted it. It was good. James relaxed. He raised his glass to Sarah. "I am happy to be here."

Sarah laughed at him. "Can I have some too?"

James poured wine for Sarah. She raised her glass, "Welcome to Scotland!"

The soup was beef and barley. It was delicious. Then Fiona brought out a mutton stew with potatoes and cabbage. James couldn't stop eating. Sarah was right. Fiona was a very good cook.

They finished the bottle of red wine.

"Shall I open the white wine?" James asked Sarah.

"Not for me. I'm tired and I have had enough to drink."

"What did Len say to you? I couldn't understand him."

"He said that the bar was full. Murder is good for business. Everyone was buying drinks for his cousin. He doesn't think we should go in there after we have finished eating."

"His cousin?"

"Oh, Jim Rumble, the fisherman who found the body. He's Len's cousin."

James stared at Sarah. "Is everyone in this village from the same family?"

"No, but most people are connected. It's a small place. Everyone knows everyone else. You can't have any private life if you live in a village like this."

"Shall I ask Fiona to make some coffee?" asked James.

Just as he spoke, Fiona came into the dining room from the kitchen.

"I made you some burnt cream. Do you want coffee?"

"Oh Fiona," said Sarah. "The meal was delicious. I don't think I can eat any more."

"Of course you can. You need to eat a lot. Food is good for you after a bad day. Do you want coffee? I know Len told you not to go into the bar. Everyone will want to ask you more questions. You should go out for a walk. Walk along by the loch. Do you want coffee first?"

"No thank you Fiona," said Sarah. "The meal was delicious and I will eat the burnt cream. But I don't need coffee. How about you James?"

"No coffee for me. I will enjoy the dessert though. What is burnt cream?"

"Eat it and find out," Fiona smiled and went back into the kitchen.

The burnt cream was an egg custard with caramel on top. It was very good.

When they finished, Sarah took the plates and wine glasses into the kitchen. They went upstairs to get jackets. It was September, and it would be cool down by the water.

They went out through the kitchen into the car park. It was full. They could hear a lot of noise from the bar. Len was right. Murder was good for business. Sarah and James walked down to the water.

"I'm confused," said James. "Is this the ocean or a loch?"

"It's a sea loch," Sarah explained. "There are a lot of them along the west coast of Scotland."

It was now 9:00pm. The sun had set but there was enough light to see. They stopped and looked at the fishing boats tied up for the night. The water was very calm and the sky was dark blue. It was very quiet and very beautiful.

"Do you know this is the first time I've been to Scotland?" said

James. "If I had known how beautiful it was, I would have come sooner."

They turned away from the village and walked along the rocky shoreline. James took Sarah's arm. "Are you OK?"

"Yes. I'm OK. Fiona always makes me feel cheerful. The meal was good, wasn't it?"

"It was excellent. But I don't think I could eat such a big meal every night. I would become as big as Len."

"I wish I knew why that man was in my garden. It seems very strange," said Sarah.

"Try not to worry about it now. Peter Duncan will come to see you in the morning. Maybe he will tell you more then."

"Yes, I know. I will have to wait until the morning. Maybe Peter will know everything. Then we can go back to my house, and you can enjoy your holiday."

James and Sarah walked for another ten minutes. Then they turned back and returned to the hotel. They went quietly to their rooms.

James fell asleep as soon as he got into bed. It had been a very tiring day.

5. MORE MYSTERY

Sarah and James ate breakfast in the hotel kitchen. Fiona had cooked bacon, eggs and sausages. James enjoyed them very much. Sarah looked pale and tired. She didn't eat anything, but she drank two cups of Fiona's excellent coffee. After breakfast they sat in the bar. It was empty. Len and Fiona were cleaning. Len gave James a newspaper to read. Sarah sat and stared out the window. At 10:00 Fiona came into the bar with Peter Duncan. He sat down opposite Sarah and James and put a folder on the table. Fiona sat down too.

"Fiona! This has nothing to do with you. Go away!" Peter said to his sister.

Fiona was annoyed. "I want to know the news!"

"Go away. This is police business. I am sure Sarah will tell you everything after I've gone."

Fiona went back to the kitchen. She closed the door very loudly.

"Where is Rory?" asked Sarah.

"I wanted to talk to you alone. We have a lot more information now. I don't understand it. I hope you can help," answered Peter.

"So you don't believe Sarah killed the man?" asked James.

"No, I don't. But my boss doesn't agree with me. I am afraid it is going to be a difficult time, Sarah."

Fiona came in with coffee and more of her homemade shortbread. Peter waited until she had gone out of the room.

"Where are your father's guns, Sarah?" he asked.

"I sold them after he died. He had a lot of rifles, shotguns and handguns. He loved hunting, and he collected old guns as well."

Peter looked at Sarah. "We searched everywhere. We found a rifle in the small river near your house. It was your father's."

"How do you know?" asked James.

"It had his name on it," answered Peter. "His name was written in gold letters on the gun, 'Andrew Dundas, Dunbarry Manor'. That was your father's name wasn't it, Sarah?"

Peter and James looked at Sarah. Her face was very white.

"But…" she said. Then she stopped.

"What is it, Sarah?" asked James. "You look shocked."

Sarah shook her head. She wouldn't say any more.

Peter and James tried to get Sarah to talk. She wouldn't say anything.

Peter gave up. He told James everything they had found out.

"Richard Wilson. Nickname: Rocky. Age: thirty-seven. Lived in Glasgow. He was a buyer and seller of antiques. He did not have a good reputation. The police in Glasgow think he was a criminal. Even if he wasn't a criminal himself, he was very friendly with people who are."

"What about the other man in the bar on the night of the murder? Fiona told us. They had an argument. Do you know about him?" asked James.

"Yes. Rory spoke to Len, and to the other customers from that night. They couldn't tell us much. The man was much older. From his accent, they thought he came from England. No one heard his name. Len gave him a cup of coffee in the morning. The man thanked him. He got into a car and drove away. No one can remember what kind of car it was. They say it was small and white or silver. That information is not useful. There are many cars like that in Scotland."

"How about the murder weapon? Are you sure it was the rifle that you found in the river?"

"We are waiting for test results. But, yes. I think Richard Wilson was shot with that rifle; the rifle with Sarah's father's name on it. The killer was standing about 50m away. He or she was not in the garden of Hill House. The person who used the rifle was standing in the field behind the house. And whoever it was, was a very good shooter."

"So that's why you don't think Sarah is the killer," said James.

"No, that's not the reason. Everyone knows that Sarah is very good at shooting. When she was young, she was quite famous."

James didn't say anything. He also knew that Sarah was good with guns. He had remembered this during their adventure in Italy in the spring. He had given Sarah a handgun and a rifle then. Peter was right. Sarah could have shot Richard Wilson. But he was sure she hadn't.

Peter spoke again. "The reason I don't think Sarah is the killer is because I know her very well. I am sure she could shoot someone, but I don't think she would go out in the dark, go into the field behind the house, and then shoot someone in the back. Also, she says she never heard anything. She was probably using her earphones at the time of the shooting. If she was trying to make us believe it was someone else, why didn't she say she heard the sound of the rifle shot?

"But my boss doesn't know her. And there is another piece of evidence. The Glasgow police did a good job. They found out a lot about where Richard Wilson had been in the past few weeks. A month ago, he went to an art exhibition in Glasgow. There was a photograph in the newspaper."

Peter Duncan took a piece of paper from the folder in front of him. He put it on the table. James looked at it. It was a copy of the photograph from the newspaper. A group of people were standing in front of a painting. One of the people was Sarah. There was a man with long dark hair standing next to her. Peter pointed to the man.

"That's Richard Wilson. Sarah said she didn't know him. But she's standing right next to him."

"But that doesn't mean anything!" James was very worried. "There were probably many people there. He is just standing next to her."

"Maybe," said Peter. "But my boss feels differently The Glasgow police talked to Richard Wilson's neighbours. About two weeks after the picture was in the papers, Richard Wilson went away. He told the neighbours he was taking a trip to the north of Scotland. No one saw him after that. We don't know where he went, or what he did, until he arrived here two days ago. He drank with another man in the bar here, they had an argument, then the next morning he was found dead in Sarah's garden."

Peter and James turned and looked at Sarah. She was pale. She was looking out of the window. James didn't think she was listening to their conversation.

James drank some coffee. "I have a question to ask you," he said to Peter.

"What's that?"

"You are telling me a lot. You are telling me everything you know, and you are telling me what you think. Why?"

"Well, you could prove you were in Italy when Richard Wilson was murdered. But in a murder investigation we have to check on everything. You might not be the murderer, but you might be connected. So I checked up on you too."

"And…?"

"I found out a lot about you. Police Headquarters spoke to the Diplomatic Service and the British Secret Service. You have had an interesting life, Mr James Winchester. People have very good things to say about you."

"That was a long time ago. These days I am a simple Counsellor in the embassy in Rome. I am going to retire soon."

"I don't think you are such a simple man. You have done many things in your life. I think you can help me. My boss wants to arrest Sarah. She knows something about that rifle we found. She won't tell me. But maybe she will tell you. Please try to get her to talk." Peter gave James a business card. "Here are my contact details. You can call me anytime."

Peter's mobile phone rang. "Excuse me," he said. He listened carefully. He looked very angry. "We will be there as soon as possible!"

He closed the phone and said, "We had a local policeman watching Hill House last night. The man must be an idiot! Rory has just called to say that someone entered the house during the night. And the policeman who was guarding the house never heard or saw anything!"

6. IS ANYTHING MISSING?

James took Sarah by the arm and gently pulled her to her feet.

"Come on Sarah," he said quietly. "Someone has broken into your house. We have to go with Peter."

Peter went into the hotel kitchen and spoke to Fiona. He came back. "Fiona is getting Sarah's handbag and jacket. She'll be back in a minute."

Fiona came running in. She helped Sarah put her jacket on. She hugged her. Fiona looked very worried, but she didn't say anything. Peter and James took Sarah out to James' rental car.

"I'll follow you up the hill," James told Peter.

When they arrived at Hill House, Rory was standing at the gate. Peter and James parked their cars. Peter came to James' car.

"Wait here with Sarah," he said.

"Why do we have to come back here?" Sarah asked James.

"Peter wants to know what was stolen. We will go into the house, and you can check."

"OK." Sarah was quiet, but she seemed a bit more relaxed.

"Sarah. You must tell me about your father's rifle. You know something about it, don't you? That's why you got such a terrible shock when Peter told you the police had found it."

Sarah turned towards James. "I will tell you. I promise. But not now."

Rory came through the gate and towards the car. "The boss says, 'Can you come and look now?'"

James and Sarah got out of the car and walked towards the house.

It looked normal. The sun was shining, and everything was very quiet and peaceful.

"How did you know someone broke into the house?" James asked Rory.

"I came up here early this morning. The local policeman was sleeping in his car. I woke him, and we went into the house. It was a mess! Then we saw the kitchen window. It was broken. I guess the thief got in that way."

There was a young policewoman standing in the hallway.

"I'm Angela Biggins," she said to Sarah. "I'm here to help you look at everything. We can tidy up as well. It's very important we find out what the thief stole."

"Thank you," Sarah smiled.

"We'll start in your bedroom," said Angela. "It's not as bad as the living room."

Sarah and Angela went upstairs. Rory disappeared. James heard a car drive away.

"Come in here, James," Peter called from the living room. The living room was big. It had a wide fireplace and big windows that opened into the garden. The furniture was old, but it looked very comfortable. There were bookcases along one wall, and a big desk in the corner. It seemed that Sarah used the room as her office. All the books had been pulled out of the bookcases, and everything from the desk was on the floor. The desk drawers were open.

"What do you think?" Peter asked James.

"It wasn't a robbery," answered James. "Those paintings on the wall look valuable. The television and video player are still here. I think whoever broke in was looking for something special."

"I agree. I think the person was looking for papers or documents. Only Sarah can tell us if the thief found what he was looking for," said Peter. "We will have to wait."

"Can't the police check for fingerprints?" asked James.

"It would be nice. But I don't think we will find anything. Rory asked the experts to come and check the area around the window in the kitchen. They said that the newest marks were from someone wearing gloves."

"I'm going to look around," James said to Peter. "I promise I won't touch anything."

Peter nodded and went out into the garden. James could see him talking on his telephone. After about twenty minutes, Sarah came downstairs with Angela.

"All my jewellery is there," said Sarah. "I can't find anything missing."

"We should check in here," said Angela.

"I can help," said James. Peter came in from the garden. He watched while Angela and James picked up books, and Sarah told them where to put them. There were hundreds of books. It took a long time. When all the books were back on the shelves, Sarah said, "I'm not sure. But I don't think any books are missing. It's hard to remember, I have so many."

Then Sarah checked her desk. "I don't think the thief took anything," she said.

"Come with me and walk around the room," said Angela. "Maybe the thief took something else."

Angela and Sarah walked around the room. Then they went into the dining room and the kitchen.

It was 1:00pm when Sarah said, "I don't think anything is missing. I don't know why someone broke into my house. But I don't think they took anything."

"Could we have a cup of tea?" asked Peter.

"I'll make it," said Angela.

Sarah, James, Peter and Angela sat in the kitchen and drank the tea.

"Well Sarah," said Peter. "I'm sorry the police guard went to sleep. I'm sorry someone broke into your house. But there's some good news too. My boss was sure you had a panic attack and killed the man in the garden. Now, he thinks that there is a bigger mystery. You and James can come back and stay here at the house. We will leave a police guard outside. But I am sure James will protect you very well. You will be safe.

"Angela and I will go now. Try to relax. We'll find out what happened. We'll find out why Richard Wilson was in your garden, and why someone killed him. And we'll find out who broke into your house."

Sarah thanked Angela. "You made it very easy," she said. "Before you go, let me show you my garden. I'd like to give you some flowers."

James walked out to the road with Peter. He guessed that Peter wanted to talk to him.

"It was very difficult to persuade my boss to let you and Sarah come back here. I lied to Sarah. My boss still thinks she is the killer. But I took a risk and called the Chief Constable. He grew up near here. He knows me, and he knows Sarah. His name is Archie Ross. He says he knows you too."

"Archie!" James was pleased. "I would love to see him! We worked together around thirty years ago. And he became a policeman!"

"Not now, James." Peter was very serious. "I told Archie that Sarah is hiding something. I also told him that maybe she would tell you. So, he agreed that you could come back to Hill House. He called my boss. My boss is very angry with me, but I think Sarah will tell you what she knows."

"OK. I understand. And Peter, thank you for believing in Sarah."

Angela came out the gate with a large bunch of roses. She got into Peter's car. Peter shook James' hand. "Call me!" he said. Then he got into his car and drove away.

James went back into the house. Sarah was in the kitchen.

"Are you hungry?" he asked Sarah.

"I didn't eat any breakfast," answered Sarah. "Yes, I'm hungry."

"Why don't you go out into the garden? I'll make us a picnic."

James made sandwiches. He found a bottle of wine and glasses. He found a picnic blanket and a basket, and put everything into the basket. He took the picnic lunch outside. Sarah was sitting on the grass in a corner of the garden.

James spread the blanket on the grass. He put down the picnic basket.

"We must talk," he said. "But first you should eat."

From the garden of Hill House, they could see the sea loch. Far out to sea, James could see the fishing boats. The sky was grey, and the water in the sea loch was rough. But it wasn't cold in the garden of Hill House.

Sarah ate some sandwiches and drank a glass of wine. Then she looked at James.

"I know I have to tell you about Davie," she said.

"Who is Davie?"

Sarah didn't answer. She drank some more wine. She didn't speak for a few minutes. Then she said, "When Peter told us they had found my father's rifle, I knew who had killed the man in my garden. I have to tell you about Davie. Then perhaps you will understand why I didn't tell Peter."

7. DAVIE

Sarah and James sat on the picnic blanket in her beautiful garden. Sarah was looking at the view. She didn't look at James.

"My childhood home is in the north. We will go there. It's about five hours drive from here. It is very beautiful but there aren't many people. There's a long narrow loch. My father's family had owned most of the land around the loch for a hundred and fifty years or more. It is not like the loch here. It's a long, thin lake. At one end there's a village. There are a few farms there too. A road from the village goes down the west side of the loch. There are no farms there. Just forests and open land. At the end of the loch there are only two houses. One is very old. It's on the edge of the water. It's called End House. About a kilometre back from the loch is a huge house. It's only about a hundred years old. My great-grandfather built it. It's called Dunbarry Manor. My father and I lived there with his mother.

"My father loved the lifestyle. He enjoyed shooting birds and hunting deer. He went fishing in the loch and in the rivers. He managed the farms and the forests. He was always busy.

"My father owned the land End House is built on too, but a family called Dumbarton had lived in the house for hundreds of years. The family I knew was a husband and wife with two sons. Mr Dumbarton was a schoolteacher. He taught at the school in the village at the other end of the loch. They had two sons. I married the elder son. Alec was twelve years older than me. I didn't know him when I was young because he was so much older, and he was always away at school. He was clever. He won a scholarship to a school in

Edinburgh. Then he went to university. He studied to become an accountant and then got a job in a bank in the city. The other son was named Davie. He is the same age as me. Davie didn't go to the village school. Davie is a little different from other people. School didn't suit him. He's very clever, but he has some strange ideas. Davie stayed at home with his mother. He wasn't happy indoors. He stayed outside most of the time. He didn't like being around a lot of people. Sometimes I met him when I was riding or walking, and then he talked to me. Davie can get very angry, very quickly. But he was always gentle to me.

"When I was twelve, my grandmother died. My father sent me to boarding school. But then, my father was lonely. He spent time with Davie. He taught him about guns. He taught him about hunting and fishing. They spent a lot of time together. Davie's father was dead by then. Davie loved my father. They were always very happy together.

"When you disappeared from Paris, I went back to Dunbarry Manor. My father was ill with cancer. Everyone knew he would die. When my father got too ill to go outside, he gave Davie his favourite rifle. It was the one with his name on it. The rifle was very important to Davie. It was his treasure. He would never sell it or give it away.

"Davie was part of my childhood. He was also my husband's brother. I feel responsible for him. I don't know why Davie killed Richard Wilson, but I think he did. I don't know why he threw my father's rifle in the river. I don't know anything. I can't tell Peter about Davie until I understand what happened.

"I want to go to End House. I want to find Davie. I want to hear his story. Then I will tell the police."

Sarah and James packed the picnic back into the basket and went back into the house. Sarah made some coffee, and they sat in the living room. It was late afternoon.

"Will you come with me to End House?" asked Sarah. "Will you help me find Davie?"

James was not sure. He had promised Peter he would find out what Sarah knew about the rifle. Now he knew that Sarah's father had given the gun to Davie. Davie was not a normal person. He might be dangerous. Sarah thought Davie had killed Richard Wilson while he was standing in the garden of this house. Then he had thrown the rifle in the river.

James thought he should tell Peter Duncan. Peter was a policeman.

He would be very angry if he knew that both Sarah and James were keeping secrets.

"Let me think about it, Sarah," he said. "You should tell the police about Davie and the rifle. I understand how you feel, but in the end, you will have to tell the police."

8. THE OTHER MAN

Fiona telephoned from the pub.

"Peter says you will stay in your own house tonight. But you have to come down to get your bags. And I have cooked for you. Be here at seven."

James and Sarah drove back down to the pub. There were some tourists eating in the dining room, a family group and two American men.

Once again, the food was delicious. There was cold potato soup, venison with a sauce made from plums, and an apple tart.

Fiona was busy. But when she had served dessert and coffee, she came and sat at their table.

"Thank you, Fiona," said James. "You are a master chef. That meal was as good as any meal I could eat in Rome or Paris."

"It should be better," said Fiona. "Everything in that meal was local. I'm pleased you enjoyed it. I like a man who likes to eat."

Just then Len came into the dining room. He was carrying a mobile phone in his hand. His hand was so big you could hardly see the phone. He started talking. Once again, James could not understand him.

Sarah translated. "Remember Fiona told us that there was a man in the bar with Richard Wilson? They had an argument and Richard Wilson left the bar. The other man got very drunk and fell asleep. Well, the people here drink a lot, but they don't fall asleep in public bars. The man went to sleep on the floor. The local fishermen thought it was very funny. One of them took a photograph of the man using his mobile phone."

Len moved next to James and showed him the photograph on the telephone. The man was asleep on the floor of the bar. He was quite fat and had a baby face. He looked about 60 years old.

"You must tell the owner of this phone to show this photograph to the police," James told Len. "I think it is very important."

Len spoke again. James was getting better at understanding him. James heard "Sarah … thought she should see … maybe she knows him … help Sarah."

Len showed the photograph to Sarah.

"No," said Sarah. "I don't know him. Make sure the police see it, Len. James is right. This man knows why Richard Wilson came to my house. I'm sure of it."

She stood up. "The meal was great, Fiona. Thank you. I am feeling much better. This is James' vacation. He should meet some local people. I'll take him to the bar and he can meet everyone."

Fiona went back to the kitchen and James and Sarah followed Len into the bar.

The bar was full of people. Even though it was September, most of the local people in the bar were wearing rubber boots, sweaters and woolly hats. The two Americans had followed them. They looked uncomfortable. They went and sat at a table over by the window.

"Sarah!" Everyone started shouting, but Fiona appeared at the door and shouted louder. "Not now! Give the poor woman some peace. Let her have a quiet drink!"

There was silence.

Len didn't ask Sarah and James what they wanted to drink. He took a bottle from under the bar and poured two whiskies.

An elderly man came over and spoke to Sarah. He pointed to a quiet group sitting near the Americans.

"Excuse me, James," said Sarah. "There are some friends over there I must talk to."

She walked away and James sipped his drink. It was the best whisky he had ever tasted. He told Len so. Len smiled.

"Len?" asked James. "Who is the man who took the photograph?"

Len pointed further down the bar. James was still having trouble understanding Len, but he understood it was the man in the green woolly hat, standing in a small group. They seemed to be fishermen.

James went to talk to him.

"Hello. I'm James Winchester. I'm staying with Sarah."

"Oh, yes. We know that," said the man in the hat. "You arrived here at an interesting time."

"Yes. I want to find out what happened. Were you all here in the pub the night of the murder?"

"Yes," said one of the men. "We were all here."

"What happened?" asked James. "I know you told the police, but I hope you will tell me too."

The men all talked at once, but it seemed that there was nothing new to learn. The two men had come into the bar. They had sat at the table where the Americans were sitting now. They had drunk whisky. They had an argument. No one heard what the argument was about.

"Who was sitting at the table next to them?" asked James.

"Old Mr Ross, Charlie Duncan and Andy McClellan. But they wouldn't have heard anything. Mr Ross is about ninety years old and he doesn't hear much. Charlie and Andy were watching a soccer match on the TV and shouting at the referee."

James was disappointed. "And then the younger man walked out?" he asked.

"Yes that's right. The other one continued drinking whisky until he fell off his chair onto the floor."

"Thanks for your help," said James. "I hope the police can do something with the photograph you took. Maybe they can send it around Scotland and ask the police everywhere to look for the man."

"They don't have to do that," said the first man. "They can find him here. He was here this morning."

"Here at the pub?" James was very surprised.

"No, no. But I saw him this morning. I was working on my boat down by the loch, and I saw him. He drove past me in his little white car."

"Where was he going?"

"I don't know. But it was the same man. I'm sure of it."

James told Len to give the fishermen a drink. He left some money on the bar to pay, and went outside onto the street.

He was worried. Had the other man broken into Sarah's house? Would he try again? Was Sarah in danger?

He took Peter Duncan's card from his pocket and called him on his mobile phone. Peter answered.

"James. Thanks for calling. Do you have anything to tell me?"

"I don't know if they have told you about this yet. But the other man, the man who was in the pub with the murdered man. There's a photograph of him, and he was seen near the village this morning."

James explained about the fishermen.

"Thank you, James. I'll send Rory McClellan to talk to them," said Peter. "Now, has Sarah told you anything?"

James didn't want to answer Peter but he knew he must say something.

"Yes," he said.

"Well what was it? Tell me."

"I don't want to tell you now. But believe me. Sarah did not kill Richard Wilson. And she doesn't know why he came to her house, or why her house was broken into."

Peter was angry. "James! You have to tell me everything you know!"

"I don't know anything, Peter. Just that Sarah didn't kill Richard Wilson. I think she might be in danger. If the other man is still near here, he might break into the house again. I want to take Sarah away."

"Where?"

"The answer to this mystery seems to be in the north. It seems to be something to do with Sarah's husband."

"He's been dead for fifteen years!"

"I know. But Sarah thinks we'll find the answers at End House. That's where she and Alec used to live. She wants to go there."

"But my boss will never agree! I'm in trouble already. My boss thinks Sarah should have been arrested!"

"I know, Peter. So I want you to give me Archie Ross' phone number. I will see if he can help us."

Peter gave James the number. He wrote it down.

"I'm very sorry about this Peter. But at least you have some more information about the other man. I'll call you as soon as possible."

James called his old friend Archie Ross. They talked for a long time. Archie agreed to help. He would tell Peter's boss in Oban that Sarah was in danger. He'd tell him that Sarah and James were leaving the area. Archie knew where they were going, but he wouldn't tell anyone. James would ask Peter to say nothing.

"Thank you Archie," said James finally. "We must get together when this mystery is solved."

"I'd like that," said Archie. "But be very careful. This might be dangerous. And look after Sarah!"

9. ALEC

James and Sarah left her house early the next morning. They took Sarah's car. It was old, but it was bigger and more comfortable than James' hire car. Peter had sent a policeman to watch the house. The policeman was sitting outside in his car. He waved to them as they drove down the hill on their way to Oban.

James enjoyed the trip. Once they were north of Oban, they drove through almost empty countryside. They drove alongside many lochs. It was very wild and very beautiful. They stopped at the Invergarry Hotel for lunch and walked around the historic town for a few minutes.

"We're less than two hours away now," said Sarah.

"Shall I drive?" asked James. "You must be getting tired."

"I'm fine. But sure, if you want to drive, please do. The roads will get much steeper and narrower from here. Is that OK for you?"

"I've driven on many mountain roads in Italy. I'm sure these can't be worse."

They left Invergarry and drove for about an hour along the side of one loch, and then another. Sarah told James about the long and exciting history of the area. They stopped now and then for James to take photographs. Then Sarah told James to turn away from the main road onto a much narrower road. Sarah stopped talking.

"Are you worried?" asked James.

"No, not really. But I am wondering what we'll find out when we get to End House."

"Tell me about Alec," said James. "You said you didn't know him when you were young. When did you meet?"

"Mrs Dumbarton, Alec and Davie's mother, knew that my father would die from cancer. She had cancer too, but she didn't tell anyone. She was worried, that there would be no one to be with Davie. She told Alec he would have to give up his job in Edinburgh and come back to End House. Alec didn't want to do this, but he knew that Davie could never live in Edinburgh. So he did what his mother asked. He came back here. Mrs Dumbarton died very soon after that.

"It was a very bad time for me. I was so much in love with you. I thought that you loved me, but you just disappeared. One night we were drinking wine together on your balcony and listening to music, then the next day you were gone."

"I explained about that," said James. "I never meant to leave you, but I got orders to go on an urgent mission. I wasn't allowed to tell anyone anything. They said it would be two or three weeks at the most. Then I got trapped in Cambodia and was in hiding for almost a year."

"I know that now, but I didn't know it then. My father finally told me that he had cancer, so I left Paris and went home. I was trying to look after my father and run the estate. Alec was living in End House with Davie. He didn't have a job, so he came every day to help me. He was kind and I was lonely. I didn't think I would ever see you again. So when Alec asked me to marry him, I said yes. My father was very pleased. He was happy that I would not be alone, and that there would be someone to look after Davie.

"Alec, Davie and I lived in Dunbarry Manor until my father died. Then we closed up the house. It was too big, and it was expensive to heat. It needed a lot of repairs too. Alec and I moved into End House. We managed the estate. Alec didn't like deer stalking or shooting birds, but he liked fishing. I got a job teaching in the village school. Davie lived with us, of course. But we didn't see him very much. He would disappear for days walking in the hills. He always carried my father's rifle.

"My father wasn't a rich man. He owned a lot of land, but that was all. Alec and I didn't have much money. I sold most of the paintings from the house and my father's gun collection. I wanted to sell Dunbarry Manor too. A company wanted to buy it. They planned to make the manor into a country hotel with golf courses and new cottages in the grounds. Alec thought it was a bad idea. He said my father had not been dead for very long. It was wrong to sell my home, even if I wasn't living in it.

"So we didn't sell it. A few years later, another group of people offered to buy Dunbarry Manor and the land around it. I thought it was a good idea, but Alec became very upset and angry. He said that Davie could never leave End House. So I went to the company and said that I would sell them Dunbarry Manor and the land, but that I would keep End House. They said that was OK, but they wanted to make the road by the loch wider. It was too narrow. Alec would not agree. He was so angry and upset, I gave up."

"How many years had you been married then?"

"About six years."

"And you didn't have children?"

"No. Of course, when we married I thought we would have children. It was only after we were married that Alec told me he didn't want any children."

"Poor Sarah! Why didn't Alec want children?"

"He believed that the Dumbartons had bad blood. He said that for hundreds of years, there had been many children in the Dumbarton family who were strange. He said he didn't want a child who was mad."

"Crazy? Like Davie?"

"We never said that Davie was mad. He's not crazy in the normal way. He's very clever. He's just different."

"So you agreed not have children?"

"I was young, and I thought Alec would change his mind. But he didn't."

"Why didn't Alec want you to sell the old house and the land around it?"

"I don't know. But the second time I tried to sell it, when we had been married for six years, he frightened me. By then our marriage was very bad. When you and I met in Italy, after so many years, I told you I had married Alec. I told you we had been married for twenty-five years when Alec died. But I didn't tell you that for most of that time, it was a very unhappy marriage.

"Alec often didn't talk to me for days or even weeks. As the years went by, he got stranger and stranger. He stopped managing the estate. He had always liked reading, but he started to read more and more. He used to spend days reading. When we closed up Dunbarry Manor, we left all the furniture in it. The library was full of books. Alec spent days in the library of the house. Sometimes he didn't come back to End House. He slept on the library floor."

"Did you ask him what he was doing?"

"Yes I tried. Usually he didn't answer. Or he would say things like 'old sins cast long shadows' or 'we can never escape our past'. Eventually I stopped asking."

"It sounds like you had a terrible life."

"My marriage was terrible, but the rest of my life wasn't so bad. I had my job at the school. I liked the children, and I liked teaching. I was busy too. When Alec stopped managing the estate, I did it myself. And of course, I had friends in the area. I would go to parties and dinners with them. After the first few years, Alec never came with me. But that was OK.

"Not long before Alec died, the government built a hydroelectric power plant on another loch nearby. They put in new roads. It was possible to get to Dunbarry Manor from the east side of the loch. It was much more convenient. There is a good road all the way from Inverness.

"When Alec died, I got another offer, and I sold most of the estate. But I kept the land with the old road on the west side of the loch, and I kept End House. When I moved away, I told Davie he could stay in End House. I haven't seen him for a long time, but I'm sure he's still living there."

10. IS ANYONE THERE?

"We're going to see Davie at End House?" asked James.

"Yes. I'll ask him what happened."

"Do you think Davie might attack you?" James was still worried.

"No. Davie would never attack me or hurt me."

"But he might shoot someone else."

"What with? He doesn't have a gun now."

"He could get another one."

"I don't think so. The gun laws in Scotland are very strict. You have to have a licence. I'm sure Davie never got a licence for my father's rifle, but he'd have to get one to buy another gun. That's a lot of paperwork. Davie wouldn't do that. And anyway, I don't think any government officer would give Davie a licence. He is not normal enough."

James sighed. "I don't like this, Sarah. We don't even know if Davie will be at End House. If he murdered Richard Wilson, he was 250km away just three days ago. And I guess he doesn't drive a car."

"No, of course not. But Davie can always find a way to do something if he wants to."

They came to some crossroads. "If we go to the left, we'll come to the village. We'll turn right. This is the road down the west side of the loch," said Sarah.

The road ran along the side of the loch. The loch was about 10km long and very narrow. About halfway along the side of the loch, the road turned away from the water. James drove up a very steep hill. At the top of the hill Sarah said, "Stop the car for a minute."

"But I will have to stop in the middle of the road! There is nowhere to pull over."

"There won't be any cars here. No one will come here. It will be OK," answered Sarah.

James stopped the car and they got out.

Sarah took James' arm and they walked to the edge of the road and looked down. The road was very steep. At the bottom of the hill, the road turned, ran along by the water for a short distance and then curved away back into the hills. There was a house between the road and the water.

"That's End House," said Sarah. "You can't see Dunbarry Manor from here."

James stared at End House. It looked very old. It was made from stone. One part was tall and narrow. It was like a square tower. The rest of the house was single storey. The windows of the tall part were very small. It stood at the very end of the loch, looking across the water.

"Long ago, the oldest part of the house was a castle," said Sarah. "Well, a farmhouse really. There were so many battles in those times that farmhouses were built to act as castles as well."

They got back in the car and James drove very slowly and carefully down to the edge of the loch. There was a rough driveway from the road down to the house. James stopped the car behind the house. Sarah got out and walked to the door. She put her hand on the door handle.

"Stop Sarah!" called James. "Don't surprise Davie. Knock!"

Sarah turned around and laughed. "If Davie is here, he will know someone is coming. He can hear a car from miles away."

Sarah went into the house and James followed. They walked through the silent rooms. It was very dark and very old, but everything was clean and tidy.

"He's not here," said Sarah sadly. "I wonder where he is?"

"If he was near your house when Richard Wilson was murdered, maybe he's not back yet." James was happy Davie wasn't there. James did not want to meet Davie. "Let's go to the village and find somewhere to stay. We can come back tomorrow."

Sarah agreed and they went back to the car. Then James had an idea.

"Sarah. Can I see Dunbarry Manor? Can we go and look?"

"The road hasn't been used for fifteen years but we can try."

James turned the car around and drove back up to the road. The road continued a little way along by the water and then turned back towards the hills.

"It's about a kilometre from here," said Sarah.

The road was narrow but it seemed in good condition. It stopped at a pair of huge iron gates. The gates were open. James stopped the car and they stared across the grass at the big old house. It looked beautiful in the afternoon sun. The gardens looked tidy, but the house had a strange empty look.

"I don't think anyone is living here," said James. "Let's drive in."

He drove up to the wide front door of the house. He stopped the car and got out. Sarah didn't move.

"Don't you want to come and look through the windows? I'll ring the doorbell first to make sure no one is at home."

Sarah didn't move. "No. You look. I have a bad feeling about the house. Maybe there are too many ghosts."

James rang the doorbell. He could hear the bell ringing through the house but it seemed there was no one there. He walked around and looked in the windows. The furniture was covered in sheets. It didn't look like anyone had been near the house for a long time, but the garden was very neat and tidy. It was strange. On one side of the house there was a room with big windows overlooking a small river. These were the windows of the library. The furniture in this room was not covered with sheets, but it still didn't look like the room had been used for a long time, except for a vase of flowers on a small desk near the window. The flowers looked about a week old. They were not fresh, but they were not dead either.

James went back to the car. He got in and drove back out the gate. Then he stopped again.

"Sarah. I thought you said there was a new road from the other side of the loch. Where is it?"

"I don't know. The government built the road to the hydroelectric power plant. The owner of the house had to pay for the driveway from the road to this house. Look – you can see the new road over there."

James looked to where Sarah was pointing. The new road was

very close, but there was no driveway connecting the house to the road, only a narrow footpath and a little wooden bridge across the river.

"It seems whoever bought the house didn't put the extra driveway in," said James. "I'm so hungry. Let's go to the village and find somewhere to eat, and somewhere to stay."

11. THE SAME MAN

They took the steep road back up the hill and down the other side. When they were driving along by the loch, they saw a car coming towards them. The road was very narrow, so James slowed down. It was small white car. James could see the driver clearly as he passed.

"Sarah! It's the man from the pub!"

"What man?" Sarah was confused.

"The man who had the argument with Richard Wilson in the pub. The one who drank too much whisky and fell asleep. I'm sure of it. You saw the photograph as well. Didn't you think it was the same man?"

"I'm not sure," said Sarah. "I didn't really look at the man in the car. But he must be the new owner of Dunbarry Manor. There's nothing else on this road. Just the two houses at the end."

It took about twenty minutes to get to the village. It had only a pub, a few shops, a church and a school.

"Where can we stay?" asked James.

"There was a bed and breakfast hotel. I hope it's still there. And I am sure they will serve some kind of food at the pub."

The bed and breakfast hotel was still open for business.

"I know the owner very well," said Sarah. "Jean is the same age as me. It will be great to see her again."

James parked the car outside and they went in.

There was no one at the front desk, so Sarah rang the bell and called out.

"Anyone here?"

A woman came down the stairs. "Can I help you?"

She walked towards them. Then she saw Sarah.

"Mrs Dumbarton! This is wonderful. I can't believe you're here!"

Sarah stared at the woman. "Millie! My goodness!"

"James, this is Jean's daughter Millie. I taught her when she was about ten or eleven years old!"

The two women started talking and laughing. "Do you remember…..What happened to Billy…My mother met an American tourist…Are you still teaching…retired…"

James was tired and hungry and bored. He didn't know who or what the two women were talking about.

"Do you have any rooms?" he asked loudly. "I am sorry to be rude, but it has been a long day."

"Sorry," said Millie. "Yes, we have rooms. It is my hotel now. My mother lives in America."

She took keys from behind the front desk and walked upstairs, still talking to Sarah. James followed.

"I'll put you in these two rooms. Can you share a bathroom?" Millie asked.

"That will be fine, thank you," James answered.

"We only do breakfast here, but you can get a meal at the pub. The food isn't very good, but it's cheap."

They went to the pub. Everyone knew Sarah. They were delighted to see her. Sarah seemed happy to talk to everyone. But James was puzzled. This was Sarah's home village. She had gone to school here, and then later she had taught in the same school. But it seemed that no one had seen her for fifteen years.

Why did Sarah never come back? he wondered.

It was almost midnight when James went to bed. He was very tired, but he couldn't sleep. He had a lot to think about. He had spoken to some of the people in the pub about Dunbarry Manor. He asked who owned it now. No one knew. They told him that an agent paid some local men to keep the garden tidy, and the road open. But they had never seen the owner.

He asked about the man in the small white car.

"Oh him!" said the barman. "His name's Walter Ferrington. He came here to live about five years ago. He's from England. He rents a small cottage at the edge of village."

"He's not very popular," said a woman standing next to James. "He's always asking questions about old stories."

"Old stories?" James was puzzled.

"You know, the stories from hundreds of years ago."

"We have a lot of stories here," said another woman. "But we don't talk about them with strangers. They are our stories. Especially, we don't tell Englishmen."

"I think he's a treasure hunter," said the first woman. "I've seen him out around the loch with a metal detector. You know, those machines people use to find old coins and buried gold."

"None of that around here," laughed the barman. "He's wasting his time."

12. JAMES IS SURPRISED

James and Sarah drove back to End House very early the next morning. Mist was still rising from the loch. Everything was grey and black and white.

"It will be a beautiful day," said Sarah. By the time they had driven over the hill and down toward the end of the loch, the day was warming up, and the greens and blues of the loch and the trees around it were appearing from out of the mist.

James parked the car at the back of the house and they walked into the kitchen.

A man was sitting at the table. Cups and saucers, and a plate of shortbread were carefully arranged in front of him.

"The tea should be ready. Will you have a cup?" he asked.

"Davie. This is my old friend James."

"Yes, I know that," the man at the table replied. "Now sit down and I will pour the tea."

Sarah sat down, but James remained standing. He stared at Davie.

He had imagined Davie to be a very big man with long hair. Probably not very clean. He had thought that Davie would not speak very well.

The man at the table was quite small. He had fading pale ginger hair, very neatly cut, and a pointed beard. He was dressed in an old fashioned suit. And he spoke like an English professor.

"James!" Sarah whispered.

James sat down, and Davie poured tea.

"I'm sorry I wasn't here when you came yesterday. It took me longer than I thought to get back."

"So you were in Beautore?" asked James

"Oh yes. I was there."

"How did you get there and back?" James wanted to know.

"I got rides in trucks and I walked some of the way."

James drank some of his tea. It was Darjeeling. It was delicious.

"Davie," said Sarah. "Why did you go down to Beautore?"

"I knew Walter Ferrington and that other man were going to break into your house. I wanted to protect you."

"Why? Did you think they were dangerous?" asked Sarah.

"Oh, the man with the long hair was dangerous. I could see he was greedy. People like that are always dangerous. Walter Ferrington is weak. Weak men can be dangerous too."

"Davie?" asked James. "Did you kill Richard Wilson?"

Davie poured the last of tea from the teapot into his cup. "Was he the man in Sarah's garden?"

"Yes," Sarah told Davie.

"Then yes, of course I killed him. Did the police find your father's rifle?"

"Yes they did, Davie. That's why James and I came here to talk to you," said Sarah.

"I'm sorry I threw it in the river but it seemed like the best thing to do."

James thought the situation was very strange. *I am sitting at the kitchen table, drinking tea with a man who looks and sounds like a retired professor, and he is very calmly telling me he killed Richard Wilson.*

"I'll boil some more water and make a new pot of tea," said Davie

He filled the kettle at the kitchen sink and put it on the stove to boil. He rinsed out the teapot, and spooned tea leaves from an old tin container with a picture of a deer on it.

"Davie," said James. "If you killed Richard Wilson, you must go to the police."

"I suppose so," said Davie. "But then they would send me to prison. I don't think I would like prison."

"So what are you going to do?" asked Sarah.

"I am thinking about that. There are things I have to tell you. I must tell you before anyone talks to the police. But I don't know how much to tell you. When I have had another cup of tea, I will go for a walk. I don't think well when I'm inside."

The water boiled and Davie made more tea. He and Sarah talked about the weather, the new trees alongside the loch, and how good the fishing was this year.

Then Sarah said, "Tell us about killing Richard Wilson."

"Very well. But I am not sure you will understand. Walter Ferrington met the younger man. You say his name is Richard Wilson. They met in the garden of the big house."

"Dunbarry Manor?" asked James.

"Yes. I was there. I hid and listened to them. Walter Ferrington said he had searched everywhere in the big house, but there was nothing. They agreed to go to Sarah's house and search there. I was worried, so I went to Beautore too. I hid in the field near your house and waited. The younger man came. I could see well in the moonlight. Sarah was downstairs. I could hear music, and I could see a light. The man stood at the window watching Sarah. He was there for a long time. The light downstairs went out. The man walked around the outside of the house. After a while he came back to the window. Then he took a hand gun from his pocket. I decided I should do something. I can move very quietly, but I was sure he would hear me if I tried to come close to him. So I thought I would shoot him. My plan was to shoot him in the arm, but I missed and the bullet hit him in the back." Davie looked puzzled. "Shooting men must be different from shooting deer. I usually never miss. Perhaps I was nervous. I had never shot a man before."

"Why did you throw the rifle in the river?" asked Sarah.

Davie looked surprised that Sarah would ask this. "But, Sarah! I had done a terrible thing. I had killed a man. I had used your father's gun. He wouldn't want me to keep it, would he? It has a man's blood on it now."

He stood up. "I'll go for my walk now. I don't know when I'll come back. Sarah, you'll find eggs, cheese and bread in the pantry for your lunch. It is late in the season, but I caught some trout for this evening, and there are some potatoes I dug from the garden at Dunbarry Manor as well."

Davie took a hat from a peg by the door and a walking stick, and disappeared.

13. THE CURSE OF THE DUMBARTONS

After lunch, James and Sarah walked out to the front of End House. A rowboat was tied to a small jetty, and someone had built a long wooden seat along the edge of the water. They sat there and looked out over the loch. It was a beautiful summer's day. But James felt uncomfortable. The old house was just behind him, and he felt like it was a monster waiting to jump on them. He shook his head and told himself not to be so stupid.

"Sarah, last night in the village, they were talking about Walter Ferrington. The man who was in the pub at Beautore with Richard Wilson. They said he is always asking questions, and that he seems to be hunting for treasure."

"Oh, him." Sarah did not seem to be very interested. "Millie said the same thing. She said he moved to the village from England a few years ago. His house is full of history books and old papers. Pity he wasn't here when Alec was alive. They might have been friends."

James was annoyed. He had so many questions. He didn't know where to start. Sarah didn't want to talk, but James wanted answers.

"When I looked in the windows of Dunbarry Manor, it seemed that no one had been there for a long time. But there were flowers in the library. Someone must have put them there in the last week or so."

"I guess Davie put them there," answered Sarah.

"Why?" asked James.

Sarah didn't answer. James was getting very angry. He looked at Sarah. *She is so beautiful,* he thought. *I loved her forty years ago, and I am sure I love her now. But I must have some answers. She told Peter Duncan that she had no secrets. I was surprised. Now I know she has many secrets. Why won't she tell me?*

He tried again. "I realised in the bar last night that you have not been back here for fifteen years. You left when Alec died. You have so many friends here, but you didn't come back. Why? How did Alec die?"

Sarah reached out and took James' hand but she didn't look at him. She sighed.

"I'm sorry. I have never talked about Alec's death. I guess I should tell you, but I'm afraid. I don't know what you will think of me."

"Sarah! I love you. I could never think badly of you!"

"I am not so sure. But I will have to tell you."

She stared across the loch for a while. Then, she started to speak.

"Alec killed himself. He hung himself in the library of Dunbarry Manor. I guess that's why Davie puts flowers there."

"Why doesn't he put them on Alec's grave?"

"There is no grave. Davie found Alec. He came and told me. Davie said it would be better if people thought it was an accident. So I drove up to Dunbarry Manor and we put Alec's body in the car. We put him in that boat and rowed out to where the water is deepest. Davie had brought stones. He filled Alec's pockets with stones, and we put him in the water. He sank to the bottom. We rowed back and then I went back out onto the loch alone. We had put Alec's fishing rod and fishing basket in the boat. I threw the oars in the water. Then I swam back to the shore."

"Why didn't Davie do it?"

"Davie can't swim. Alec couldn't either. I called the police and told them that Alec had not come back from a fishing trip. They searched and they found the boat and Alec's fishing rod. They never found his body. After it was all over, I went to stay in the village with Jean, Millie's mother. I was quite ill. Jean made me stay in bed for about a week. Then a lawyer came, and said there was someone who wanted to buy Dunbarry Manor and all the furniture. I owned the house, not Alec. So I could sell it. I signed the papers. Then Davie came and said he thought I should go south. 'Go to Hill House,' he said. 'It will be better for you'. So I packed clothes, books and a few photographs and moved to Beautore. I got a job teaching in a school not far away. I made a new life. Now, maybe you understand why I never came back."

James was shocked. "Do you think the police and all the people in the village believed you?"

"I don't know. A lot of people knew that Alec was very difficult. And of course, most people in the village know the history of the Dumbarton family. Maybe they thought he had drowned himself. But no one ever said anything."

"When the woman in the pub last night was talking about old stories, did she mean stories about the Dumbarton family?" asked James.

"This area has a long history. There are many stories. But yes, the curse of the Dumbartons is one of them."

"So Walter Ferrington has been asking questions about the Dumbartons. We saw him coming here. So he is interested in Dunbarry Manor or End House, or maybe both! That is the connection between you and Richard Wilson and Walter Ferrington."

"No one in the village will tell him anything. He can read what is in the books, but that's all."

"What is the curse of the Dumbartons?"

Sarah let go of James' hand. She stood up and turned away from the loch. She stared at End House.

"It's a very old house. Dumbartons have lived here for hundreds of years. Old houses and old families often have lots of stories. But there is only one story about this one." She shivered.

"Are you cold? Shall we go inside?" asked James.

"No. No, I couldn't talk about this inside the house. It's quite difficult, even out here in the fresh air and sunlight. It's a long story, so please be patient."

She sat down again next to James.

"The story is that long ago, in the 12th or 13th century, there was war between two chieftains. Different storytellers use different names but I'll call them Morgann and Domnaill. The leader of the people in this area was Domnaill. He had a younger brother named Cullen, and a wife called Eva. Domnaill was killed in a battle. Cullen thought that the people would then choose him as leader. But the people didn't like him, so they chose their priest as their leader. Cullen was very angry. He wanted revenge. Sometime later, the people heard that Morgann was planning to attack them again. The priest knew that Morgann was stronger than them. The priest didn't know anything about war. He didn't know what to do. He asked Cullen for advice. Cullen said they must protect the children. All the children must be hidden. The priest was the leader, but he listened to Cullen, and he believed him. They took all the children from babies to about ten years old, and some women to look after them. They hid them in a cave in the valley behind where Dunbarry Manor is now. The villagers covered the entrance with rocks and trees. Then Cullen went to Morgann and told him about the children. He said that if Morgann paid him, he would show the soldiers where the children were hidden. Morgann gave him money, and Cullen went with the soldiers and showed them the hiding place. The soldiers killed everyone. They killed the women with swords but they carried the children down here to the loch and drowned them. The soldiers forced Cullen to watch. But the story says that he didn't care.

"When Eva heard about this, she was very angry. She was very angry with Cullen. She cursed him. She said that he had taken the children away from the people. He had sold the children for money. She said that he must learn what it was like to lose children. But it was too easy if his children died. Eva said that Cullen's children and their children, and all the children born to his family in the future, would be cursed. There would be children in every generation who carried Cullen's curse. They would live long lives, but they would have bad blood. They would be mad. In this area, all the Dumbartons are descendants of Cullen. So people say they carry the curse."

"And people still believe this?" James was amazed.

Sarah shrugged. "I don't know what people believe now. But there are a lot of stories about mad Dumbartons. They are just stories, but Alec believed them. As I told you, that's why he didn't want to have children."

"Because of Davie? Because Davie is different?"

Sarah shrugged her shoulders again. "Maybe. But I think with Alec there were other reasons too."

14. WALTER FERRINGTON

James stared across the water. He did not know what to say to Sarah. She seemed to feel that all these stories about curses and killing children and wars were normal. He wondered why Davie had persuaded Sarah to put Alec's body in the loch. And why Davie had told Sarah to go south to her grandparents' old house in Beautore. Nothing made any sense.

Then James heard a car. It was far away, but the sound travelled across the water. Someone was coming.

"Sarah! Is there a place I can hide the car? There's someone coming and I don't want them to know that we're here."

"Why?"

"Don't ask me now. I'll explain later. Just tell me where I can hide the car."

"There's nowhere here. You'll have to drive up to Dunbarry Manor. There are garages behind the house. You should be able to hide the car somewhere there. But you will have to hurry!"

James ran to the back of the house. The keys were still in the car. He jumped in and drove away from End House as quickly as he could. He hoped the driver of the other car would not hear him. He thought it would be OK because the hill was between him and the other car. The garages were locked, but he was able to park the car behind an old stone building. No one would see it unless they came to look. He was just in time. As he got out of Sarah's car, he heard the other car approaching the gates. James ran to the corner of the house, and hid behind a large tree. He looked out from behind the tree. Walter Ferrington had parked his car in the driveway. He was walking towards the other side of the house.

The library! thought James. *He didn't find what he wanted at Sarah's house so he's come back here to look again.*

James moved very quietly. He crept around the back of Dunbarry Manor and then up the other side of the house towards the library windows. With his back against the wall, he moved up until he could see into the library. As he was watching, Walter Ferrington pushed everything off the small desk near the window onto the floor. This included a vase of flowers. James noticed the flowers were fresh. So Davie had come in and changed the flowers.

James felt angry. Who was Walter Ferrington? He was moving the desk. He was going to lift the carpet up. Why?

James didn't know who owned the house, but he was sure it wasn't Ferrington because he had climbed in through the window. If he owned the house he would have a key for the door. James went back to the car. He looked in the boot and found a tool for changing tires. He used the tool to force open a door at the back of the house.

I'll find out who owns the house and apologise later, he thought.

The door opened into a kitchen. A tap was dripping.

Maybe Davie changed the water in the flower vase here, he thought.

He walked along the hallway until he found the door to the library. Ferrington was moving around inside. He was talking to himself, but James couldn't hear what he was saying.

James opened the door very quietly. Ferrington didn't hear him.

"There must be something. A map. Where is it? I've looked everywhere. Maybe it's behind one of the pictures. I'll cut them out of their frames. Maybe it's in End House. But I can't go there."

James slipped inside the door and crept up behind Ferrington. Then he grabbed him.

"Don't kill me! Don't kill me. I haven't got anything!" shouted Ferrington.

"Don't be an idiot!" said James. "I'm not going to kill you. But I want to talk to you."

James held onto Ferrington very tightly. He pushed him against a wall. He held the man's arm up behind his back.

"I'm not going to kill you. But if you don't answer my questions

I'll break your arm."

Ferrington twisted his body to look at James. They were about the same age, but James was much bigger and stronger. He stared at James' face.

This man knows what he is doing, thought Ferrington. *I believe him. If I don't talk, he will hurt me.*

"OK," said Ferrington. "What do you want to know?"

"Why are you in this house? What is your relationship with Richard Wilson? What are you are looking for?"

"You don't know?" Ferrington was surprised. "Then why are you here?"

"I saw you climbing in the window. This is not your house. I want to know why you are here."

"But how do you know about Richard Wilson? Are you a policeman?"

"No. I'm not a policeman, but I have friends who tell me things."

This man could be very useful, thought Ferrington. *I need help. Richard Wilson was no help at all. This man looks better. It seems he knows criminals. Maybe he can even get into End House.*

"I'll tell you everything," he said to James. "It's a good story, and there's a lot of money in it. If you help me, we can split the money."

"Tell me," said James.

"I have lived in the village here for five years now. I heard that there was treasure hidden near here, and I decided to find it. It has taken a long time and I think I am close. But I need help."

Ferrington told James the story about Cullen and Morgann. James didn't tell him he had heard it before.

"The locals say that Cullen never spent the money Morgann paid him. He hid it. They say he lived in a very small house where End House is now. The oldest parts of End House are 12th or 13th century, so it is probably true. No one in the village would talk to Cullen. They hated him, but they were afraid to kill him. Eva said he must live so that the curse would have effect. Cullen married someone. No one knows who she was or where she came from, but she had a son. When the boy was about ten years old, he started going crazy, and Cullen killed himself. Or some people say the wife or the son killed him. Anyway he died. Since then there have always been people living in End House who have gone crazy. Some murders and many suicides. But the interesting part of the story is that the secret of where Cullen hid his money is passed from father to son. Davie Dumbarton is the last. He knows where this treasure is. But he will never tell anyone."

"How did you find all this information? Is it in books?" asked James.

"No. No. But Davie Dumbarton had a brother His name was Alec. He drowned in the loch about fifteen years ago. But before he died, he spent most of his time in this room. He was collecting information about Cullen and the Dumbarton family. When I heard about that I decided to search this house. No one lives here. Men come to do the garden, but they never come into the house. It took me a long time, but I found Alec Dumbarton's notebooks. I found where he had hidden them."

"And you read the notebooks and found out where the treasure was?"

"Not really. I didn't get much information from them. It was pages and pages of notes. It seemed to be trying to prove that Cullen was a hero and the old story wasn't true. But he did write down that the secret was passed from father to son. There was a lot about sacred guardians and how the Dumbartons had promised to guard the treasure with their lives."

"But there wasn't a lot of treasure around in the 12th and 13th century. I guess Morgann probably just gave Cullen a few coins. They have probably rusted away. Why do you call it a treasure?" asked James.

"It must be a great treasure." Ferrington looked like a disappointed child. "Why else would a family guard it and keep it secret for so many hundreds of years? It must be valuable. I'm sure there is a map or something like that. I couldn't find it here. Then I heard that this house belonged to Alec Dumbarton's wife. I thought he must have given the map to her. Or she knew where it was. She took it with her when she moved away."

"Why did you team up with Richard Wilson?"

"Well, when I find the treasure it will be hard to sell. I need an antiques dealer. I was in Glasgow looking for a dealer. I talked to a lot of people. Wilson must have heard about me. He came to visit me here. He said he would help. I told him about the woman in Beautore. I said we needed to search the house, so we went there. He wanted to force the woman to tell us where the treasure was. I thought we should wait until she wasn't there and search the house. He went to the house without me. The next day I heard some fishermen talking about how a man was found dead in her garden."

"So then you broke into her house?"

"Yes. It was easy. Someone shot Richard Wilson. That was good. He can't tell anyone about the treasure now. She wasn't in the house. I had all night to look. There was a policeman outside, but he was sleeping."

"But you didn't find anything?"

"No, nothing. It was no good."

"Why didn't you search End House?"

Ferrington didn't answer, He didn't want to tell James that he had tried to search the house. He had waited until Davie went out. The house wasn't locked. It should have been easy. But when he went into the house it seemed to be very evil. He thought he could hear people talking. He became very frightened and ran away.

"The map must be there. You can help me. You can go to End House and find the map. We will find the treasure. We will sell it. Half the money for you, and half for me."

"Why are you so sure there is a map?" asked James.

"There must be a map. It's treasure. There is always a map."

James looked at Walter Ferrington.

This man is an idiot, he thought. *He dreams of buried treasure. He probably believes in fairies as well. Davie might be odd. Davie might even be mad. But this man is very strange.*

"OK," said James. "I will let you go now. Go back to the village and wait. I will go to End House. I will find this Davie that you talked about. I will see what I can find out."

"No!" shouted Ferrington. "You want to take the treasure for yourself. It's my treasure."

James pulled Ferrington's arm up his back. Ferrington screamed. James put his face very close to the other man's.

"Listen to me. I do not want the treasure. I don't believe there is any treasure. I think you are a very stupid man. Go back to the village and stay there. If I see you anywhere near this house or End House, I will break both your arms and maybe your legs as well! Now get out of here!"

Ferrington looked at James. He was very frightened. James looked very serious and very dangerous.

End House

James let go of Ferrington's arm. Ferrington ran to the window and climbed out. James waited. He heard the sound of a car being driven fast down the drive. James sat back on the sofa and laughed. He had been a diplomat for a long time. It was many years since he led a dangerous life. But he had not forgotten.

I enjoyed that, thought James. *I'm sixty-five and will retire soon, but I can still scare someone!*

15. END HOUSE AT NIGHT

James went back to End House. He found Sarah in the kitchen peeling potatoes.

"It was Walter Ferrington, wasn't it?" she said. "I watched out the window. I saw his car go by."

"Yes. It was him," James replied. "He climbed in a window and was searching the library. We had a conversation."

"And?" Sarah turned towards James.

"And he is an idiot. He has been searching for Cullen's treasure."

"What treasure?"

"He believes Morgann gave Cullen something very valuable. That Cullen hid it and left a map. He has been looking for it. He joined up with Richard Wilson because he needed someone to sell the treasure, and he wanted someone to help search your house at Beautore."

"Why has he been searching at my house and Dunbarry Manor, and not here? I agree with you. There is no treasure. But if there were, surely he would think the map or the information would be in End House."

"I asked him that. He was a bit strange about it. He was very happy for me to search this house. But he didn't want to. I wonder if he tried and Davie scared him away."

"Maybe he is scared of the spirits?"

"Sarah! Not you too! What are you talking about? Ghosts?"

"No…" Sarah didn't seem sure. "Very old houses have an

atmosphere. I think that sometimes you can feel the people who were there before. Not ghosts. But something…"

James laughed. "Well I am here now, and I can't feel any spirits or see any ghosts. When will we eat?"

"In about half an hour. There's no wine. Davie does not believe in alcohol. I might be able to find some whisky somewhere."

"Not necessary. I have a present from Len!"

James went out to the car and brought in a bottle of wine.

They ate the trout and potatoes, and drank half the wine.

"Thank you Sarah," said James. "Much better food than we ate last night."

Sarah held up the wine bottle. "More wine?"

"Oh, no. I guess we should be getting back to Millie's bed and breakfast hotel. I shouldn't drink any more if I am going to drive."

Sarah put the bottle down and stared at James. "Go back? We are staying here of course."

"Here?" James was not happy. He had laughed at Sarah about the ghosts and spirits, but the truth was, he didn't like End House.

"Yes. I am staying. You can go to Millie's if you want, but I am staying here. I checked. Davie has made up beds for both of us. This is my house. My home. I might never live here again, but I am staying here tonight."

James gave up. He would not leave Sarah alone in this house.

"OK," he said. "Where am I sleeping?"

Sarah smiled at him. "There is a room next to the living room. I think it will be OK. Davie has put sheets on the bed in my old room. Flowers on the dressing table too."

James was jealous. "The room you and Alec used?"

"No. After the first few years I never slept in the same room as Alec. I used a room at the top of the old tower."

"Can I see?"

"If you want to."

Sarah led James to the oldest part of the house. They climbed the stairs to the top. It was a very small room with a narrow window. James looked out of the window. There was a view down the loch towards the village. He shivered.

"It must have terrible for you. All those years staying in this tiny room. Didn't you feel like a prisoner?"

"No. I had my books. And I had music. I prepared my classes for school. Later I had a computer too. I liked it. It was quiet and private."

"Weren't you lonely?"

"Sometimes. Let's go downstairs."

They sat in the living room and read for a while. James found a book on Scottish history. It was not very interesting, but he understood that the Scots in ancient times went to war a lot. Finally Sarah went to bed. James drank the last of the wine and went to bed too.

The wine had made him sleepy. He climbed into the wooden bed and fell asleep almost immediately.

16. I HAVE THINGS TO TELL YOU

James woke from a deep sleep. Someone had pressed a finger against his neck.

It was Davie.

"Come outside with me," said Davie. "But get dressed first. We have some walking to do."

Davie disappeared. James got up and dressed. He found Davie in the kitchen. He was making tea.

"I have decided what to do. I have things to say. I will say them to you, not Sarah," said Davie. "But we should go outside. The house will not like me telling you these things."

"The house?" asked James. He was still half asleep, and Davie was saying crazy things.

Davie thought about James' question. "Well, maybe not the house. But the people who are in the house will be angry. We'll go outside. I don't want anything bad to happen to you."

"What about Sarah?"

"She will be safe. The only person who would hurt Sarah is Alec, and he's not here."

"Where is he? Where is Alec?"

"He's at Dunbarry Manor," said Davie. "He never left there after he killed himself."

"He's a ghost?" asked James.

Davie poured two cups of tea.

"Ghosts? No! No man! The people in this house and Alec at Dunbarry Manor are not ghosts!"

"What are they?" James drank some tea.

"Mmm. I am not sure what to say. Memories? Feelings? Anger? Something. They do not walk around like ghosts, but they are here. Many of them. So finish your tea. We will go outside."

"Won't they follow us?"

"Oh no. That is why I always liked to be outside. They do not go outside."

I must be crazy, thought James. *It is the middle of the night and I'm having this conversation. Davie sounds like a professor. He sounds normal. So when he says these strange things, I believe him.*

Davie and James walked to the edge of the loch. They sat on the wooden seat where James and Sarah had sat the day before.

Davie didn't speak, but James had some questions.

"Davie," he said. "You said that Richard Wilson had a handgun. You said you shot him because he had a gun. But the police didn't find it."

"No, of course not. I went to check him. I found that he was dead. I took his gun."

"Why?"

"Why not? I had to throw the rifle away. It was Andrew Dundas' rifle. He was not a man killer. Neither was I. I did a terrible thing. I killed Richard Wilson. I did not mean to, but I did. That made the rifle evil. I could not keep it. But I thought I might have to kill someone else, so I would need a gun."

James thought about this. He understood that this made sense to Davie. He waited, but Davie didn't say anything more.

"Davie?" asked James. "Who owns Dunbarry Manor?"

"I do," answered Davie.

"You!" James was amazed. "Why? How?"

"Because Alec had died there. I knew he would stay there. His spirit. His memory. I could not let strangers buy the house. And I knew that Sarah must leave. She had a chance at a normal life. She could not stay here. So she needed the money for the house. I bought it."

"How did you get the money to pay for it?"

"I had a lot of money. People always thought the family was poor but that was not true. The Dumbartons always had a lot of money.

The family did not live in End House because they had no money. They lived here because they could not leave. The promise and the curse kept them here."

"Where did the money come from?"

"Oh, it was nothing special. From time to time, some family member would escape. They would go to London, or later to places like Canada and Australia. Some were very successful, but they never came back. They sent money though. The families who stayed here in the house didn't spend much money. Year after year after year they saved it. They never put it in a bank. They bought gold, diamonds and silver. They hid it in the house. When Alec killed himself, the gold, silver and diamonds were mine. I went to Glasgow and I sold them. It was difficult, but I managed. Then I found a lawyer and bought the house. The lawyer did everything. I have looked after the house and the garden. I did that for Alec, but mostly I did it for Sarah's father, Andrew Dundas. He loved that house."

James had heard many strange things since he had arrived in Scotland. But he thought that this was the strangest. He looked at Davie. Davie, who everyone said was 'different'. They never said he was 'mad', but James thought that they meant 'mad'.

"You are asking a lot of questions," said Davie. "But I have something to tell you. Please listen to me."

"I'm sorry," said James. "Please tell me."

"Has Sarah told you the story of Cullen and Morgann and the children?"

"Yes, she has."

"Then you know that Morgann paid Cullen?"

"Yes."

"That man, Walter Ferrington, knew that the Dumbartons stayed in this house to guard something. He thought it was Cullen's treasure. There is no treasure. There is only Cullen's Shame. That's what we guard. I am going to show you where it is."

"Why me?"

"I am the last of the Dumbartons. I am the only one now who knows. I have to tell someone. I thought I would tell Sarah. But then I thought 'No. I will tell the Englishman, Sarah's friend. He will know what to do.'"

Davie turned to look at James. "When I met you, I knew that you were once a hunter like me. I am a deer hunter. I know everything about deer. You were a hunter in the world. You know about laws and policemen and people and money. I don't know any of those things. Come with me now. While we walk, I will tell you a story, and I will show you what is hidden."

17. CULLEN'S SHAME

Davie stood up and walked around the side of the house and up to the road. James followed him. There was some light from the moon, but not much. Davie didn't seem to need any light. James stayed close to him as they walked along the road.

"Of course, my father told Alec the secret. But later Alec had to tell me. I was thirteen. It was summer. Alec was home for a short time. He had finished university, and was about to start his job at the bank.

"One day he came to find me. He was very upset. There had been a storm. Part of the hill had fallen down. The hiding place was much easier to see from the road. Alec needed my help. There were some people with a metal detector. They were searching for metal alongside the loch. They had found the hiding place."

Davie turned towards the hill and started climbing up through the rocks and bushes. About ten metres above the road he stopped and waited for James. James joined him. Davie took a torch out of his pocket and shone the light on the hillside.

"Here it is," said Davie.

James looked. He couldn't see anything except branches and leaves. Davie pulled some branches away and then James could see a crack in the rock.

"Alec and I had to move bushes from other places to hide the entrance. I have not been back here since that day. We did a good job.

The bushes have grown well."

Davie and James cleared the branches away. A narrow iron door was set in the crack in the rocks. It had a rusty iron bar across it. Together they lifted the bar and pushed the door open.

Davie shone the torch into the area behind the door. The crack in the rock stretched back. Sometime in the past, someone had widened the crack behind the door to make a small room. As the light moved around James gasped. On the floor of the room were three skeletons. One was half buried in the soil. Davie shone the light on the other two.

These skeletons looked younger. There were traces of clothing on the bones, and part of a bag next to one of them. James looked closely. Both the skulls had holes in them. It looked like both had been hit on the head with something very heavy. Then he saw an axe by the feet of one of the skeletons.

"How long have these skeletons been here?" he asked.

"Well. I was thirteen, so that would be fifty years wouldn't it?" answered Davie.

"So these were the people who found the hiding place?"

"Yes. I don't know who they were, or where they came from. I always thought someone would come looking for them and ask questions, but no one ever came."

"What about the other skeleton?" asked James.

Davie didn't seem to be interested.

"I don't know. Someone from long ago. I didn't bring you here to look at skeletons. I brought you here to show you this."

Davie pointed the torch at the back wall. Stones had been carefully stacked to make a flat surface. On top of this was a box. It was quite small. It was made from wood with iron bands around it.

"Take a look," said Davie. "This is what I wanted you to see."

James stepped carefully over the bones and looked.

"I can't see anything, Davie. Can I have the torch?"

Davie handed him the torch, and James lifted the lid of the box. As he did so, the iron bands broke, and rust fell onto the stone. James pointed the torch inside the box. There were the remains of a leather bag. There were just a few pieces left. There were also small discs about the size of a fingernail.

"What are these round things?" James asked Davie.

"I have never looked in the box, but I know what they are. They are silver coins. They have the king's name on them. If you count them, I am sure you will find that there are thirty of them. They are Cullen's Shame."

"Why are they called Cullen's Shame?"

"When Cullen asked Morgann for money in exchange for information, Morgann gave it to him. But Morgann didn't like traitors. Cullen had sold the children. So he gave him thirty pieces of silver. Like the Romans gave Judas in the Bible.

"The story people tell each other now includes Eva's curse. But only the Dumbartons know the whole curse. Eva told Cullen that she had cursed him and everyone in his family that would come after him. She said that the money had the blood of the children on it, but so long as the money was never spent, the family line would continue. There would always be some children who could marry and have their own children. Cullen's bloodline would continue. So Cullen hid the money. He promised that no one would ever see it. Every generation since then has guarded this box. Every oldest son has promised to guard the secret and Cullen's Shame with his life."

"So why are you showing me now?" asked James.

"I am the last of the Dumbartons. There will be no children, so the curse will die. The bloodline is finished. There is nothing to hide anymore."

James stared into the box. Such an old story, and so much death, for only thirty tiny silver coins.

"Do you want me to keep the secret?" he asked Davie. Davie didn't answer. James looked up. Davie had gone.

James climbed out of the crack in the rock. He looked down the hillside and along the road. He could not see Davie anywhere. He pulled the door shut and replaced the bar. He tried to arrange the branches so the entrance could not be seen. Then he climbed down the hill onto the road and walked back to End House.

Back inside the house, James looked at his watch. It was 3:00am. He had a lot to think about. He knew if he went to bed he would not sleep. He sat at the kitchen table and thought about what he should do. He thought about what he should tell Sarah. About 4:30 he fell asleep with his head on the table.

18. DAVIE'S LETTER

Sarah woke James up. "James. What are you doing here?"
James yawned and blinked at her. "What time is it?"
"About 7:30. Have you been out?"
"Yes, I went out with Davie. Have you seen him?"
"No. But I looked out my window this morning. The rowboat is out on the loch. Maybe Davie went fishing."
James had a very bad feeling. "Sarah, are there any binoculars here?"
"Yes, probably. Somewhere. I will go and look."
Sarah came back quite soon with a very old pair of binoculars.
James went up to Sarah's room at the top of the old tower. Sarah followed him.
The binoculars were old, but when James looked through them at the rowboat, he could see very clearly that there was no one in it.
He handed the binoculars to Sarah. She looked out across the loch. Then she turned to James. Her eyes were full of tears.
"Davie is dead. He has drowned in the loch."
"I'm sorry," said James gently. "I think you are right. You told me he couldn't swim."
"No. He couldn't. It was maybe the only thing he couldn't do. He rowed out there. I guess he filled his pockets with rocks and went into the water. It's over, James. But why now?"
James took the binoculars from Sarah and put them on the bed.

He took her hand, and they walked down the stairs and out into the garden. On the wooden seat near the jetty they found two pieces of paper and an envelope weighted down by a pistol. James picked up the gun and handed the papers to Sarah. She read the first sheet in silence. Then she handed it to James. As James expected, it was a letter from Davie.

--- *My Dear Sarah,*

It is time for my life to finish. I will join Alec. You and I spent a lot of our life together, but you must not grieve. Some things are meant to be. I am pleased that the story that started with Cullen will finish with me. It is time for you to go back to Beautore. Go now. Do not wait here. There is nothing to wait for.

Poor Alec never recovered from the deaths of those people. James will explain that part to you.

Afterwards, Alec tried to prove that the stories about Cullen were not true. That's why he spent so many hours reading and searching. When he realized that most of the story was true, he killed himself. I think it was better that he did.

Trust James. I think he will know what to do about everything.

Davie---

Sarah handed the second sheet of paper to James. It was folded over with James' name written on the outside. "It's for you."

The note was very short.

---*This pistol might be useful.*---

"What's in the envelope?" asked Sarah.

"I think it is Davie's will."

"Will? But Davie didn't own anything!"

"I think he did. But now I think we should go. Come on. We will pack up and go back to Beautore."

"But we have to call the police!"

"I would rather talk to Peter Duncan and Archie Ross than to the police here. And Davie said we should go. He is dead, but I think we should do what he said."

"OK. If you say so," said Sarah.

They packed quickly. Before they got into the car, they walked along the road and James pointed to the spot on the hill where the iron door was hidden by the bushes.

"The hiding place is up there. I will tell you everything that Davie told me. But now I think we should go."

James didn't know why, but he felt that they needed to leave quickly.

At the crossroads to the village he stopped the car and got out. He took out his mobile phone and called Archie Ross, his old friend who was now Chief Constable.

"Archie. I'm in a hurry. Please don't ask questions now. I'll tell you everything later. But can you please arrange for the local police to arrest a man called Walter Ferrington? No, he's not the murderer. He's probably harmless, but I don't want him looking around and searching for a few days. The police can arrest him for breaking into a house. Thanks. We're on our way back to Beautore. I'll call you tonight."

19. HE DIDN'T DO IT

Three days later, James was at a dinner party with Sarah. Archie Ross was on vacation and had invited them to his country house about 20km south of Beautore. Peter Duncan was also at the party.

While they were eating, Archie made Sarah and Peter laugh a lot by telling them stories about what he and James had done when they were young. Peter and Sarah talked about their childhood days. It was a very pleasant evening. James felt relaxed. He looked across the table at Sarah. She was laughing at one of Archie's jokes. She was wearing a dark blue evening dress and pearls.

I have to keep her in my life, thought James. *I wonder if she will agree to come back to Rome with me?*

James could not believe that he had left Rome just seven days before. So much had happened.

James and Sarah had driven from End House to Oban and gone to the police station. They arrived there at lunchtime. Luckily Peter had been in his office. They told him everything that had happened. James gave the pistol to Peter.

Peter told Rory McClellan to go out and buy sandwiches. Someone brought them cups of very bad coffee. Peter talked to his boss, and then he had called Archie. Archie arranged for a team to go the next day to recover the skeletons from the hiding place and to search for Davie. No one believed they would find his body. The loch was very deep in places, but it was important to try.

They were in Peter's office for hours. When they finished explaining everything, Sarah and James stood up to leave.

"I'll call you when we know more about the skeletons and get some information about the pistol…" Peter was saying to them when his telephone rang.

Peter answered his phone. He listened to the person on the other end of the line. Then he said, "About lunchtime, they say? OK, I'll tell her. Please tell me if you learn anything more."

He hung up and turned to Sarah. "I'm sorry to tell you this. That was Archie. About lunchtime today someone in the village noticed smoke at the far end of the loch. They called the nearest fire station, and the villagers went to help as well. But they couldn't do anything. By the time the fire fighters arrived, End House was totally burnt. The stone walls are still standing but there is nothing else left. The fire fighters have not seen anything like it. They are saying there must have been an explosion or something in the house that could burn very hot and very fast."

James felt very cold when he heard this. Davie had told them to leave End House, not to wait. Also James had decided not to go to the local police. If he had, would he and Sarah have been in the house with the police when the fire started? Had Davie known this would happen? James didn't know, but it seemed like Davie was still looking after them.

"I don't mind," Sarah said to Peter. "I think it's better like this. Davie wanted to end the story. The house was part of the story too. Now everything has gone."

They had left Oban, driven back to Beautore, where Fiona fed them again, and then fallen into bed at Hill House. They had both slept for fourteen hours.

"James!" Archie was talking to him. "Stop dreaming! Do you want port or whisky?"

"Uh, whisky, thank you. Sorry about that. I was just thinking about everything that had happened."

"I was pleased you could identify those two skeletons," Sarah smiled at Peter. "Their families must have been very upset when they just disappeared!"

"Oh, you know who they were?" Archie was interested. "That was quick."

"We found the remains of the man's wallet near the skeletons," explained Peter.

"They were a middle-aged couple called Martin and Cheryl Watling. They were from near London. Martin Watling was a woodwork teacher. They liked to spend their holidays walking and

End House

searching for coins. They had gone on a month's walking and camping tour in the Highlands and never returned. By the time their family contacted the police to say they were missing, they had probably been dead for almost a month."

"And you found Richard Wilsons fingerprints on the pistol?"

"Yes. That confirmed Davie's story. Richard Wilson didn't have a gun licence, and the gun was probably stolen, but he had definitely handled the pistol recently."

"Everything has turned out very well," said Archie. "It was surprising that Davie owned Dunbarry Manor. Did that surprise you Sarah?"

"I'm not surprised that he bought it. It was the kind of thing that Davie would do. But I'm surprised that he had the money to buy it."

"And he left it to you?"

"Yes, I think so. When he made his will, he told the lawyer that when he died, he wanted me to have everything he owned.

"So yes, I own Dunbarry Manor again. Of course everything else he owned was burnt in the fire."

"Will you miss him Sarah?" asked Peter. "Will you miss Davie?"

"Of course, but Davie always knew what he wanted. He wanted this ending. So I should not be sad."

Peter turned to James. "You liked him didn't you?"

"Yes I did. Very much. He was a very unique person. I wish there had been more time to talk with him."

"So," said Archie. "He was a very unique and special person, who murdered three people."

"No!" Sarah put her glass down with a bang. "He didn't!"

Everyone at the table turned to look at Sarah. Sarah stared back at them.

"Davie killed Richard Wilson. He didn't mean to kill him. He just wanted to stop him because he thought Richard Wilson would hurt me. But that's all."

"But, Sarah. Who killed the Watlings? It must have been Davie!" Peter was puzzled.

"Alec killed them. I thought you all understood that. Alec found them at the hiding place. He hit them with an axe. He needed help to hide the bodies, so he went and got Davie."

Archie, Peter and James looked at each other. None of them had ever thought that Alec was a murderer. They all thought that Davie was the only killer, and that Alec had tried to protect him.

Archie put his hand over Sarah's. "Oh, dear. This is very hard for you isn't it? Are you sure?"

"Of course I am sure. It probably doesn't matter, because they are both dead. But I want you to understand. Davie was not a violent person."

"You're right, of course." Archie patted Sarah's hand. "Do you know the saying 'old sins cast long shadows'?"

"Yes," answered Sarah. "Alec used to say it sometimes."

Archie stood up. "Does everyone have a drink? I want to propose a toast."

Everyone stood up.

"To chasing away the shadows."

"And to letting the sunlight in," added James.

THANK YOU

Thank you for reading End House. (Word count: 22,898) If you enjoyed this story, you might also like On the Run, Book 3 in the Old Secrets - Modern Mysteries Series.

If you would like to read more graded readers, please visit our website http://www.italkyoutalk.com

Other Level 4 graded readers include
Chi-obaa and Friends
Chi-obaa and Her Town
On the Run (Old Secrets – Modern Mysteries Book 3)
The Blue Lace Curtain (Old Secrets – Modern Mysteries Book 1)
The Legacy
The Witches of Nakashige
Vanished Away

ABOUT THE AUTHOR

I Talk You Talk Press is a Japan-based publisher of language textbooks, graded readers and language learning/teaching resources.

Our team is made up of highly experienced language teachers and translators, who have all studied at least one additional language to an advanced level.

This experience enables us to design our materials from the perspective of both the teacher and the learner. We consult with both teachers and language learners when designing our textbooks and graded readers, and test our materials extensively in the classroom before publication.

We are a fast-growing press, and currently publish graded readers for learners of English. We publish new graded readers monthly.

www.ingramcontent.com/pod-product-compliance
Lightning Source LLC
Chambersburg PA
CBHW032210040426
42449CB00005B/523